JOURNEY AROUND *the* SUN

The Story of Halley's Comet

Written by
JAMES GLADSTONE

Illustrated by
YAARA ESHET

Owlkids Books

I have seen your past.

And I will see your future,
the next time I take that
sunlight journey.

Long ago, people looked up at me in wonder.

What was I? A fire burning in the sky?

Aristotle—a famous philosopher of Ancient Greece—thought comets formed close to the Earth when superhot gas in our atmosphere burst into flames.

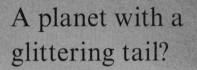

A planet with a
glittering tail?

Arab writings record that a planet with a tail
was seen for twenty-two days from the city of
Cairo in the year 989. Historians now know
that was Halley's Comet.

Some people called me a hairy star,

Eadwine, a monk who lived in medieval England, helped to create a book called the *Eadwine Psalter*. It has a drawing described as a hairy star. Scholars think this may be Halley's Comet when it was seen in 1145.

a bushy star,

Chinese astronomers saw what they called a bushy star in the year 374. This was their name for a comet with no tail. Historians today believe the astronomers had seen Halley's Comet.

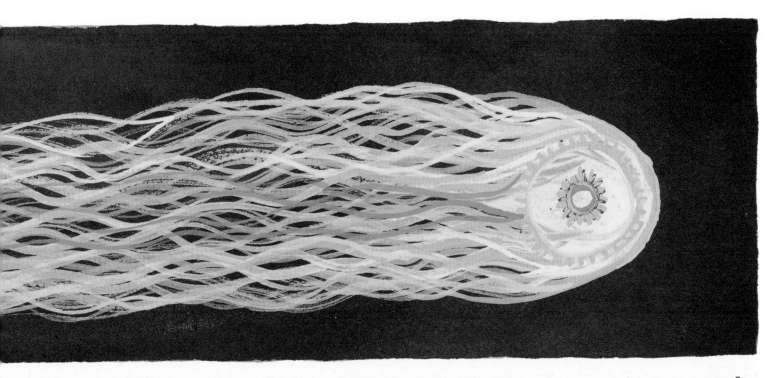

or said I looked like
a great sword of flame!

In 1607, Flemish astronomer Gottfried
Wendelin saw Halley's Comet from what is
today known as Belgium. He wrote that the
comet looked like a flaming sword.

One person said my tail was like a peacock's, fanned out in a long, proud trail.

When Halley's Comet returned in 1456, Italian astronomer Paolo Toscanelli thought the comet's tail looked like a peacock's stretching across the sky over his home in Florence. (We see Halley's Comet in our night sky when it travels close to the Sun, about every seventy-five to seventy-six years. When this happens, we say the comet returns.)

For centuries, I was a mystery, woven through human history in drawings, paintings, and words.

Chinese astronomers have recorded each return of Halley's Comet (except one) since 240 BCE.

Ancient Babylonians set down astronomical observations on clay tablets. They noted Halley's Comet as far back as 164 BCE.

Italian artist Giotto painted Halley's Comet as the Star of Bethlehem in a famous fresco called *Adoration of the Magi*. He may have seen Halley's Comet during its return in 1301.

In a portrait of fifteenth-century German astronomer Regiomontanus, he holds an astrolabe—a device used to estimate distances between Earth and objects in space, including comets.

So often you saw my light as a messenger of misfortune. But I am only a comet, neither good nor bad—a part of nature.

Your thoughts were so fearful, full of old superstition.

Halley's Comet returned in 1066, just a few months before the Battle of Hastings. King Harold of England died in this battle, an event that was woven into the Bayeux Tapestry along with an image of the comet.

Each time I returned, no one knew it was me— the same comet orbiting the Sun.

No one knew, that is, until 1758, when I returned as Edmond Halley had predicted.

Sir Edmond Halley was an English scientist who lived from 1656 to 1742. Halley's mathematical calculations suggested that comets seen in 1531, 1607, and 1682 were actually the same comet orbiting the Sun. In 1705, Halley published a book called *A Synopsis of the Astronomy of Comets*, in which he predicted that the same comet would return again in 1758.

When Halley was a young man, he saw the comet during its return in 1682. The comet would come to bear his name years later, when his calculations proved to be correct.

Amateur German astronomer Johann Palitzsch was the first to observe Halley's Comet on Christmas Night in 1758. Though Sir Edmond did not live to see his prediction come true, the comet returned right on schedule.

Now that you could predict my next bright return,
I became the star of a once-in-a-lifetime show.

On hillsides and shoulders—even up in a
balloon—you watched me blaze toward
the Sun.

During the 1910 return of Halley's Comet, one daring American scientist—David Todd—took a hot-air balloon up hundreds of feet to view the comet more clearly through a small telescope. Todd knew that Earth's atmosphere causes distortion when viewing the night sky. The higher up you go, the less distortion there is.

New photographic
cameras captured my
flight. Look at me—
heated up and speeding
through the frame!

During the 1910 return, photographs
helped people see more clearly what
the comet looked like. Thousands of
photographs were taken, many from
cameras mounted on telescopes.

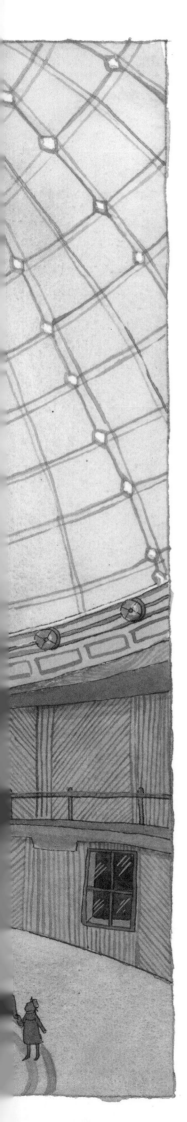

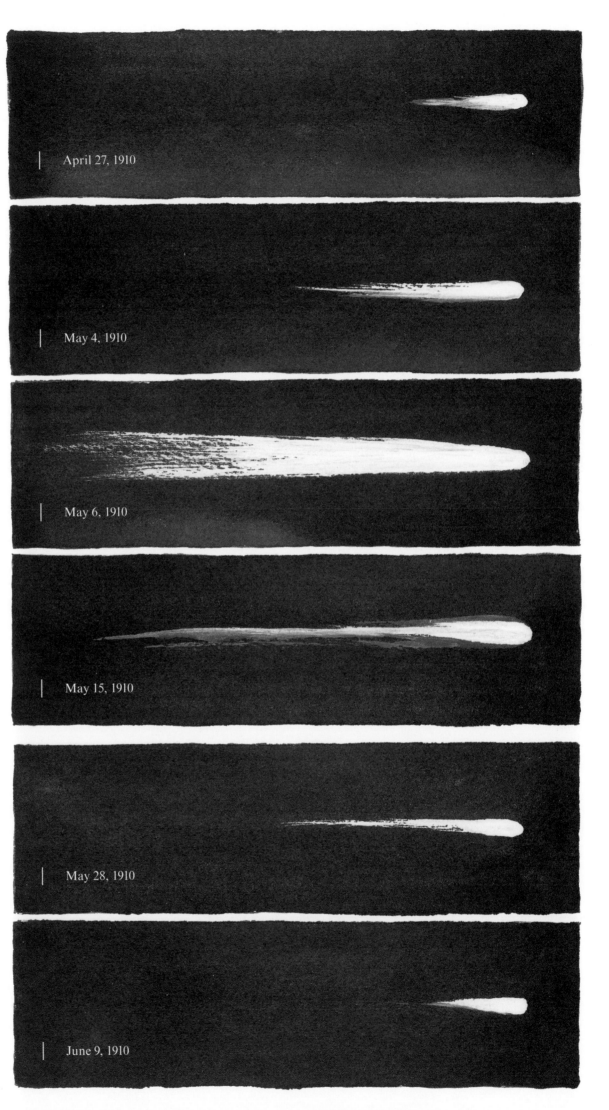

April 27, 1910

May 4, 1910

May 6, 1910

May 15, 1910

May 28, 1910

June 9, 1910

Then came the space
age and Giotto—
a spacecraft! It came
to see me at very
close range.

When Halley's Comet returned in 1986,
scientists were ready. Several space
probes—known together as the Halley
Armada—were launched to gather data
to be sent back to Earth. The Giotto
probe—named after the Italian artist—
came within 370 miles (595 kilometers)
of the comet.

Now I am traveling through the
cold, dark reaches far from the Sun,
my tail disappearing.

As Halley's Comet journeys away from the Sun, it travels toward
aphelion. Aphelion is the point of orbit at which an object is most
distant from the Sun. Halley's Comet reaches aphelion past the
planet Neptune—close to 3 billion miles (4.8 billion kilometers)
away from the Sun! From that distance, the Sun appears about
thirty times smaller than it does from Earth.

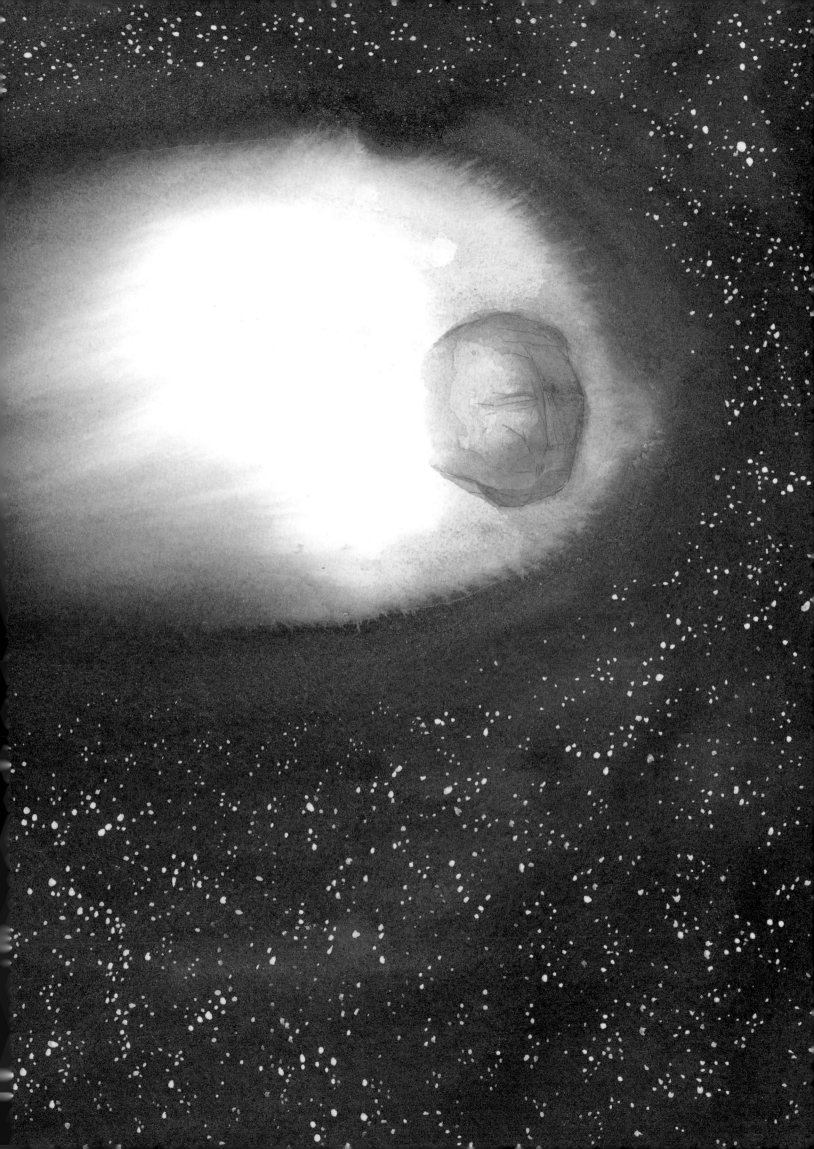

But I will return to you,
the next time I take that
sunlight journey.

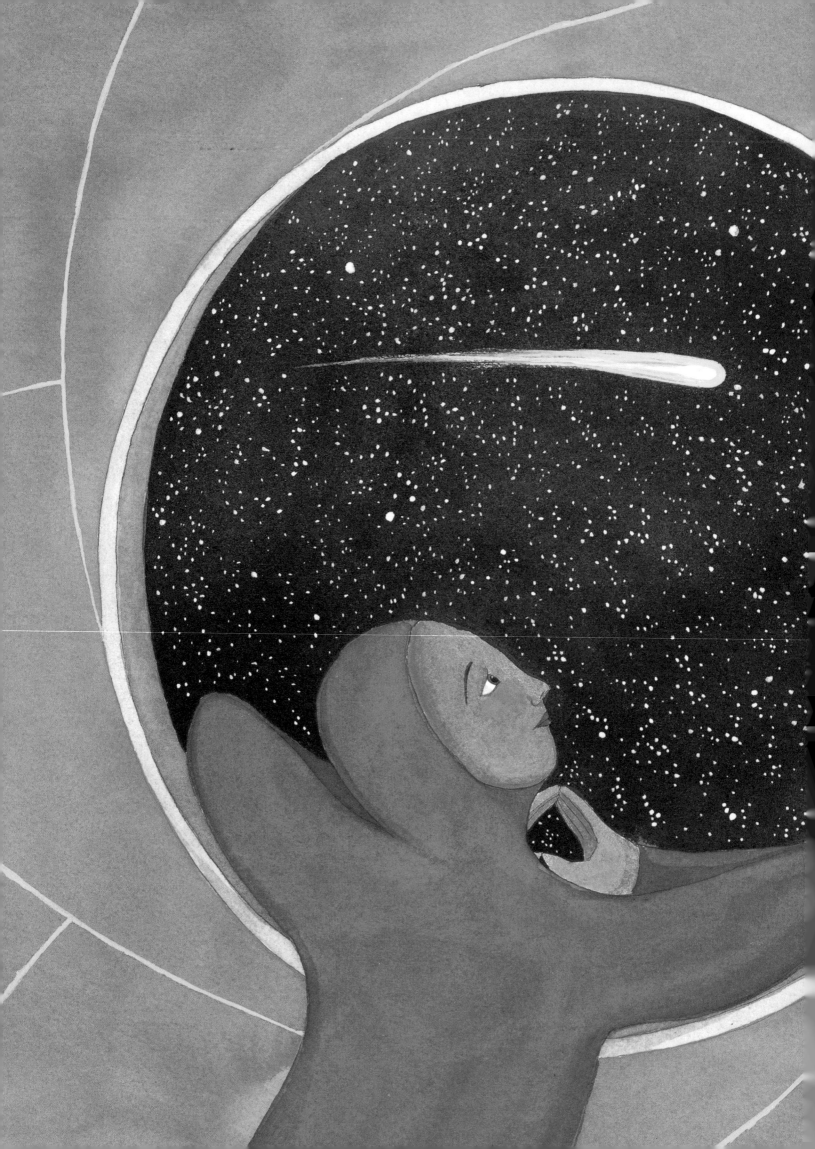

Will you watch out for me?

A Note from the Author

Have you ever seen a comet light up the night sky? There's a good chance you will see one during your life. You will probably even see Halley's Comet! That's because Halley's Comet goes around the Sun about every seventy-five or seventy-six years, making its appearance in our sky—its return—a once-in-a-lifetime event. (A few lucky people may see Halley's Comet twice in their life.) And even though the comet may look like it is in our sky when it returns, it is still millions of miles away from Earth.

I saw Halley's Comet in 1986, when I was a young man of sixteen. I may see it on its next return to the inner solar system—in 2061—but only if I live to be a very old man.

I wrote *Journey Around the Sun* as though Halley's Comet could see, think, and speak—which of course it can't. But if the comet could see, it would have witnessed remarkable changes in humanity over thousands of years: the rise and fall of ancient civilizations; new technologies, such as telescopes, to help us see objects in space; and the rise of modern science, which helps us to appreciate comets for what they really are—rather than fearing them as bad omens.

There have been other comets that were brighter and more spectacular than Halley's Comet. But it is the most famous comet because it's the first one whose orbital return was correctly predicted.

What changes in people's lives and to planet Earth do you think Halley's Comet will see as it visits us over the coming centuries?

WHAT ARE COMETS?

Comets are ancient objects that orbit the Sun. The word "orbit" means to go around. Each comet takes a different length of time to make one full orbit. Short-period comets, like Halley's Comet, take anywhere from a few to two hundred years to orbit the Sun. Long-period comets complete their orbit in two hundred to many thousands of years.

A comet is made up of ice, frozen gas, dust, and rock—together these are called the nucleus. A comet's nucleus is much smaller than any of the planets in our solar system. As a comet travels closer to the heat of the Sun, some ice and frozen gas boils off the nucleus, carrying some dust off, too. This forms a coma—a cloud of gas and dust that surrounds the nucleus. Some comas grow to be thousands of miles across in size.

The tail also forms as the comet travels closer to the Sun. A comet usually has two tails—one of gas and one of dust. Comet tails often put on dazzling displays, growing to millions of miles in length!

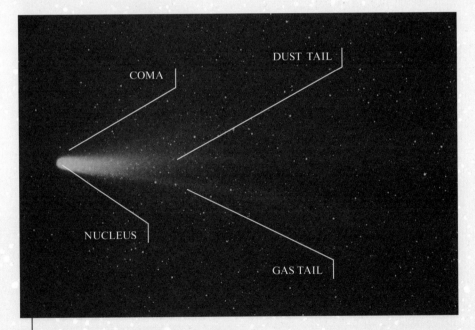

HALLEY'S COMET (MARCH 8, 1986)

For Mom, always a delighted watcher of the night sky
— J.G.

To my parents, Tsipora and Levi
— Y.E.

AUTHOR'S SOURCES

Karam, P. Andrew. *Comets: Nature and Culture*. London: Reaktion Books Ltd., 2017.

Lancaster-Brown, Peter. *Halley and His Comet*. Dorset, UK: Blandford Press, 1985.

Levy, David H. *Comets: Creators and Destroyers*. New York: Touchstone, 1998.

Moore, Patrick, and John Mason. *The Return of Halley's Comet*. London: W.W. Norton, 1984.

Sagan, Carl, and Ann Druyan. *Comet*. New York: Random House, 1985.

Stephenson, F.R., and C.B.F. Walker, eds. *Halley's Comet in History*. London: British Museum Publications, 1985.

Text © 2021 James Gladstone
Illustrations © 2021 Yaara Eshet

Owlkids Books acknowledges the financial support of the Canada Council for the Arts, the Ontario Arts Council, the Government of Canada through the Canada Book Fund (CBF), and the Government of Ontario through the Ontario Creates Book Initiative for our publishing activities.

Published in Canada by Owlkids Books Inc.
1 Eglinton Avenue East, Toronto, ON, M4P 3A1

Published in the US by Owlkids Books Inc.
1700 Fourth Street, Berkeley, CA, 94710

Library of Congress Control Number: 2020939444

Library and Archives Canada Cataloguing in Publication
Title: Journey around the sun : the story of Halley's comet / written by James Gladstone ; illustrated by Yaara Eshet.
Names: Gladstone, James, 1969- author. | Eshet, Yaara (Illustrator), illustrator.
Identifiers: Canadiana 20200259407 | ISBN 9781771473712 (hardcover)
Subjects: LCSH: Halley's comet—Juvenile literature
Classification: LCC QB723.H2 G53 2021 | DDC j523.6/42—dc23

Edited by Karen Li & Stacey Roderick
Designed by Alisa Baldwin

Photo credit: page 31, courtesy of NASA

Manufactured in Guangdong Province, Dongguan City, China, in September 2020, by Toppan Leefung Packaging & Printing (Dongguan) Co., Ltd.
Job #BAYDC84

A   B   C   D   E   F

ONTARIO ARTS COUNCIL
CONSEIL DES ARTS DE L'ONTARIO
an Ontario government agency
un organisme du gouvernement de l'Ontario

Canada Council
for the Arts

Conseil des Arts
du Canada

Canada

Publisher of Chirp, Chickadee and OWL
www.owlkidsbooks.com

Owlkids Books is a division of **bayard** canada